Original title:
Dolphins in the Breeze

Copyright © 2025 Creative Arts Management OÜ
All rights reserved.

Author: Jameson Hartfield
ISBN HARDBACK: 978-1-80587-408-9
ISBN PAPERBACK: 978-1-80587-878-0

Reflections of the Unknown

In a splashy dance, they glide and sway,
Fins a-wiggling in the bright ballet.
Bubbles burst with giggles loud,
As they play pranks on the passing crowd.

A leap, a twist, a tail flipped high,
They tickle the waves as they zoom by.
With flippers flying, they spin and twirl,
Like silly acrobats in a watery whirl.

Whispers of laughter from the sea so deep,
In the midst of their games, they hardly sleep.
With cheeky grins and sparkling eyes,
They plot their next joke, oh what a surprise!

When the sun dips low and the sky turns pink,
They gather round for a giggly drink.
Sharing tales of the pranks underway,
As the waters chuckle till the end of day.

Frolics Beneath the Salted Sun

Flippers splashing, laughter rings,
Bubbles dance as mischief swings.
Sunny rays with salty hugs,
Chasing shadows, wiggly shrugs.

Popping up with silly bows,
Parking tricks like crafty prose.
With a wink, they twist and twirl,
Spinning tails in a joyful swirl.

Surging Silhouettes at Dusk

As daylight dims, they play around,
Jumps and flips, a playful sound.
Silhouettes in the fading light,
Giggling echoes of pure delight.

Chasing stars that twinkle bright,
In the water, a silly sight.
They weave and roll with hat tricks bold,
A comedy show, in waves uncontrolled.

Graceful Spirits of the Tide

Gliding through in rhythmic grace,
Silly faces, no time to chase.
With each splash, a cheer erupts,
Water ballet, laughter stirred up.

Twirling like tops in a joyful spree,
Winking at fish, 'Come dance with me!'
Making splashes, a frothy swirl,
Ocean's jesters, in glee they whirl.

Harmonies of Wave and Air

On the crest, they leap with cheer,
Swirls of fun that all can hear.
Melodies of playful shouts,
Making waves, there are no doubts.

With each dive, a surprise awaits,
Silly antics, they tempt their fates.
Together they sing, in tunes they wean,
The ocean's jesters, forever keen.

Playful Shadows on Crystal Waves

Gliding through the gleam, they play,
Bubbles pop like jokes at bay.
Twists and turns, a watery dance,
Spraying joy with every chance.

Flipping high with glee, they show,
Splashing water, a laughing flow.
In the sun's warm, bright embrace,
They're the clowns of the ocean space.

Breezy Journeys of the Flippers

With flippers flapping, they embark,
On wild rides, leaving their mark.
Chasing waves with a grin so wide,
In the sweet ocean, they take pride.

Whispers of the sea bring laughter,
As they frolic, chasing after.
Kicking up foam, they twirl and spin,
In this boat of fun, they always win.

Crescendos in the Deep Blue

Under the waves, a symphony plays,
With whirls and swirls in playful ways.
Each leap a note, each splash a cheer,
Creating music that all can hear.

The ocean's stage, a fun-filled show,
With silly antics, they steal the flow.
Riding currents like a silly stream,
In watery dreams, they giggle and beam.

Joyful Leaps through Morning Mist

Morning light breaks, a brand new day,
Through the fog, they splash and sway.
With leaps so wild, they steal the scene,
Making waves like a playful machine.

A dance of joy, a frothy spree,
Chasing sunbeams, wild and free.
In this ballet beneath the sky,
With every jump, their spirits fly.

Airborne Harmony

The fishy friends take flight,
With flips and twirls in the sunlight.
They giggle and splash in the air,
Chasing bubbles without a care.

Sardines glance with a smirk,
As our jesters do their quirky work.
A ballet on the rolling waves,
Pretending to be ocean braves.

Playmates of the Ocean's Breath

In the salty foam they leap,
Practicing antics that make us peep.
Witty pranks on seaweed greens,
Dancing like animated machines.

With a wink, they swipe some sand,
You'd swear it was all perfectly planned.
The gulls cackle overhead,
As laughter echoes where they tread.

Enchanted Sea Choreography

Twisting in a joyful spree,
Making mischief, oh so free.
Flip and flop, dive and sway,
Creating chaos in their play.

With tails like anchors, they twirl around,
A glimpse of grace, then hit the ground.
Surfing waves like a bumpy ride,
Who knew the sea could be this wild?

Splashing in the Light

A shimmer here and a splash there,
Sudden bursts of joy fill the air.
With silly smiles and cheeky spins,
They're the kings of giggles, let the fun begin!

Floating on their backs, they bask,
Wrinkled brows, no big task.
Life's a game of leapfrog right,
Under the sun, pure delight!

Untamed Waves

On a surfboard, I made my stand,
Wobbling like a clumsy band.
Fish in the water must be the judge,
As I belly flop with a splish and a fudge!

Flippers flailing, I chase my tail,
My friends all laugh, I turn pale.
A seagull steals my sandwich treat,
As I splash around, look at my feet!

Celestial Glimpses Beneath

Bubbles dance in the ocean's sway,
I peek below at the fish ballet.
A clownfish winks, 'Oh what a sight!'
I trip on seaweed, oh what a fright!

Starfish giggle, they know my plight,
As I float like a kite, quite the sight.
The octopus waves with eight silly hands,
While a crab forever plays in the sands!

Aqua Elegance

With a flip and a flop, I glide with flair,
But my landing and rolling shows I don't care.
A porpoise snickers, 'You're quite the champ!'
As I twirl around, I look like a lamp!

In the tides, we whirl like a wacky spin,
The coral reefs cheer for the chaos within.
As I try to dunk, I miss the hoop,
And look at my pals—oh, what a troupe!

Surf Symphony

The waves conduct a symphony grand,
With splashy notes from my flippered hand.
I sing a tune with a bubbly flow,
While my seaweed wig dances to and fro!

Crabs keep the beat, as seagulls hum,
While I spin like a top, feeling quite dumb.
But laughter erupts from the watery trail,
In this oceanic chaos, we all prevail!

Delightful Waterscape

In the splash of sunny rays,
Fish do flips, in silly ways.
Bubbles float with giggles bright,
As seaweed dances, oh what a sight!

Jellyfish are having fun,
Like balloons that dance and run.
Crabs with hats, all snappy-dressed,
Throwing parties, oh, they're blessed!

Seagulls swoop with cheeky calls,
While the octopus, it juggles balls.
Underwater laughter fills the nooks,
With fishy tales from storybooks!

So join the creatures in this play,
Where sea and sun just love to stay.
With every splash, the smiles grow wide,
In this watery world, joy does abide.

Breezy Dawn Explorers

Morning breaks with giggles loud,
Sailing boats, oh, they are proud.
Waves are clapping with delight,
As they dance in morning light.

Noses diving, tails in the air,
Splashing friends, without a care.
Seashells spin in joyful glee,
As the fishes sing with glee!

A crab's ballet upon the sand,
While starfish clap; it's quite the band!
Breezes carry the fun-filled cheer,
Echoing laughter, bright and clear.

Come join our merry aquatic crew,
In every splash, we'll fit right through.
With ticklish tides and joyful chime,
We'll frolic here, it's the best time!

Flowing Through Aquatic Grace

Gliding by with frolicsome glee,
Splashing water, oh, what a spree!
Mermaids giggle and twirl with flair,
Tickled by bubbles that fill the air.

Sea turtles wearing glasses, how cute,
Chasing waves in their birthday suits!
Seashells sing a lulling tune,
While dolphins dance beneath the moon.

Fish in coats of colors bold,
Start a conga line, oh, behold!
An eel plays guitar; it strums a tune,
As they dance beneath the afternoon.

In this aquatic paradise of fun,
Every wave is a race to run.
With playful hearts and spirits bright,
Joy flows eternal, day and night.

Serenity in Motion

With a puff of wind, they take the plunge,
In graceful arcs, they brightly lunge.
Chasing waves like a game of tag,
Bouncing high with a happy brag!

In the gentle sway of morning tide,
The fish wear grins they cannot hide.
Giggling seagulls swoop and dive,
Creating ripples, oh, how they thrive!

Coral castles, bright and grand,
Are playgrounds in this wet wonderland.
A dolphin trip in the sunlit cheer,
Where laughter lingers, never fear!

So watch these creatures leap and twirl,
In this water, where joy does swirl.
With every splash, the world feels light,
In the fun of the ocean, all feels right!

Spirits in Fluid Motion

In the splash of waves, they leap and dive,
With joyful squeaks, they come alive.
They twirl and twist, a comical sight,
Like clumsy dancers in the sunlight.

They play with fish, a slippery game,
Each wiggle and wriggle, none is the same.
With a flick of their tails, they send a splash,
Turning our laughter into a dash.

Wonders of the Shimmering Deep

Beneath the sun, in waters clear,
A gang of jesters, full of cheer.
They wiggle their noses, what a great show,
Making bubbles that flutter and flow.

With every flip, they tease the waves,
Chasing the currents, like playful knaves.
They giggle in gurgles, soft and bright,
Our floating friends, in pure delight.

Rhythm of Water and Wind

In sync with the tide, they dance and play,
Bouncing around in a silly way.
With synchronized swirls that make you grin,
A frolicsome party under the fin.

The splashes echo, a watery tune,
As they spin and twirl, over wave and dune.
Their laughter bubbles to the sparkling sky,
As they share the joy, oh me, oh my!

Joyful Explorations

Through kelp forests, they zoom and glide,
Where colors swirl, their antics reside.
With cartwheels and flips, they weave a spell,
Creating a spectacle, who can tell?

They nudge at shells, exploring all day,
In search of treasures, come join the play!
With bubbly voices and tails held high,
They charm the ocean, oh my, oh my!

Nautical Serenade

In blue waves where the fish like to dance,
Silly sea critters take a crazy chance.
They wiggle and giggle, a splashy parade,
Hats made of seaweed, they never just fade.

With flips and with flops, they tease the young tide,
Juggling with bubbles, they take it in stride.
A conch shell orchestra starts up the show,
As laughter erupts from below and above.

Waves of Elegance

In a tuxedo made of dazzling scales,
They waltz through the water, no need for trails.
With a twirl and a swirl, they sip on the breeze,
Merrily spinning with stylish ease.

Fish in the front row clap their fins loud,
Cheering the pranksters, so graceful and proud.
A seaweed bowtie flutters, oh so chic,
Each leap brings a chuckle, it's laughter they seek.

Aerial Acrobats

In mid-air they flip, with a splash and a grin,
Chasing their shadows, they dive and they spin.
With tails that are whips, they ride every swell,
Telling the ocean each tale they tell.

The gulls take a gander at such a grand sight,
As the sky and the sea play tag day and night.
A pirouette here and a belly flop there,
Creates a delicious shore breeze, oh so rare.

Rhythms of the Ocean's Heart

With tunes from the tide, they dance to the beat,
Shaking their tails in a comical feat.
They strut with the waves, fueled by giggles galore,
As seagulls observe from their perch on the shore.

Each splash tells a joke only fish understand,
As crustaceans chuckle and clap in the sand.
The rhythm of laughter, the heartbeat of glee,
In this jolly kingdom, wild and free.

Gentle Giants of the Seas

In the waves, they twist and play,
Bouncing like a beach ball, hooray!
With clicks and whistles, they sing,
Wearing shells like a bling-bling.

Their smiles so wide, they'd make you grin,
In the salty spray, let the fun begin!
They surf the swells with goofy grace,
Showcasing moves, they own the space.

With a splash and a giggle, they dive,
Chasing fish like they're alive!
Gentle giants, showing their tricks,
Their underwater dance, a clever mix.

Who knew the ocean held such mirth?
A playful twist on the old earth!
In every frolic, laughter is found,
These merry mates spin joy all around.

Skimming the Surface

Sailing sideways, tail in the air,
They leap and splash without a care.
Like furry jesters of the sea,
Crafting joy that's wild and free.

They clown around, eyes full of glee,
With flips and flops, they make us see.
A merry band of happy souls,
Bound together, like swimming goals.

With playful nudges, bump and roll,
Tickling fish, that's their main goal!
Sliding over waves, in a race,
These happy friends bring smiles to the place.

Their laughter echoes through the tide,
A joyride on the ocean wide!
On skimming breaths, they'll take the leap,
Life is silly in their deep.

Glimmers of the Deep

Under the surface, a sparkling show,
Where goofy antics steal the flow.
With swirling tails and cheeky pride,
They twist and twirl, nowhere to hide.

A raucous splash and a sudden dive,
In a circus of waves, they come alive.
Bubbles like laughter fill the spray,
In every frolic, there's fun at play.

They race the current, a silly chase,
Tickling the seaweed in their space.
Charming fish with their shiny show,
These jesters of the ocean, go with the flow.

With beaming smiles, they cue the fun,
Under the waves, where giggles run!
In glimmers bright of the deep blue sea,
Joyful stories dance with glee.

Ocean's Joyous Symphony

A symphony plays in the ocean's sway,
With laughter and splashes, they start the day.
Whistles and whoops rise high in the air,
A concert of fun without a care.

As they leap and glide, in perfect tune,
Their antics make waves beneath the moon.
With joyful frolics and silly spins,
They orchestrate laughter, that's where it begins.

A tap on the water with flippers strong,
Creating tunes that say, 'Come along!'
Together they dance, a vibrant display,
With every splash, they steal the day.

In the swell of the sea, they rise and fall,
With jokes and jests, they charm us all!
In this ocean's symphony so grand,
Joyous echoes meet every hand.

Celestial Swimmers at the Edge of Light

They leap and twirl, with goofy grace,
Their antics put a smile on every face.
With bubbly giggles echoing around,
They dance in dreams where laughter is found.

Sprightly splashes, a joyful sight,
Tickling the waves, what pure delight!
They spin and dive, so full of cheer,
Making waves, spreading fun far and near.

Flight of the Sea's Merry Dancers

In the shimmering sea, they frolic and play,
With silly leaps that light up the day.
Whirling through the surf, such a lively bunch,
They party with the seashells and share a munch.

With flip-floppy moves, they whirl and sway,
Engaging in games; oh, what a display!
Caught in a splash, they giggle and grin,
Creating their own oceanic din.

Glimmering Souls Beneath the Sky

In the azure deep, they glide with glee,
Grinning at seagulls with wild jubilee.
They wear seaweed crowns and twinkle with flair,
While exchanging heckles with each curious pair.

Chasing the bubbles, they pop with a cheer,
Comedic performers, full of good cheer.
Swirling in synchrony, laughter they spread,
Beneath the sunbeams, joyfully led.

Wayfarers of the Watery Realm

Adventurous sprites with a penchant for flops,
Through coral castles, their laughter hops.
With jellyfish friends, they juggle and tease,
Spreading joy like a summer breeze.

In ocean's embrace, they twinkle and dive,
Crafting tales of whimsy, how they thrive.
They race with the currents, splashy and bold,
These jolly sea jesters, a sight to behold.

Mirthful Movements Through the Tides

In the splashy dance of the sea,
Blubbering joy looks plain silly,
Flipping tails with cheeky flair,
They giggle bubbles into the air.

With quirks that mimic a grand ballet,
They twirl and spin, then laugh away,
In their watery world, they play tag,
While seaweed sways, they snag their rag.

A splash, a leap, a playful whack,
Chasing the sun, they never lack,
Their jovial calls echoing deep,
As sandy shores get ready to leap.

Oh, what fun in the frothy foam,
They frolic together, far from home,
With each twist, they leave a trace,
In the tidal rhythm, they find their place.

Dreams of Liquid Breezes

In the swirling waves, they plot and scheme,
Wiggling through currents like a lovely dream,
Joking with each other, they swim and prance,
In a merry luau, they take a chance.

With eyes like marbles, they share a grin,
As if the ocean was made just for sin,
They leap in the air like they own the sky,
And belly flop down with a raucous cry.

Waving their fins with a silly zest,
Every splash is a jest, a light-hearted test,
They spin in circles, in water they dine,
In this watery world, they're truly divine.

Laughter echoes through coral and kelp,
I swear they can talk, if just for a yelp,
In their liquid playground, they never tire,
Spreading joy like a bubbly fire.

Harmonious Twirls under the Eternal Blue

Beneath a blanket that hugs the sky,
They whirligig forward, oh my, oh my!
In synchronized splashes, they jump like a kite,
Creating ripples that dance with delight.

They prance and they pounce on a sunbeam's ray,
Making waves giggle and squeal in the spray,
A frothy revolt, they twist and they weave,
Eying the seaweed, concocting a leave.

With a flip and a flop, they snicker with glee,
Imagining humans, trying to be free,
While teaching the fish their very best play,
In joyous mischief, they steal the day.

Drifting like clouds, with a sarcastic grin,
In the ocean's embrace, they spin andpin,
In this boundless ballet, they'll always be wrote,
Chasing each wave, in a buoyant boat.

Elation in the Wake of Waves

With the waves rolling high, they twinkle and shine,
Each crest is a giggle, a frolic divine,
They race the tide, with antics so grand,
In a splashy parade, splendidly planned.

Tumbling through bubbles, they're having a ball,
Riding the swells, oh, avoiding the fall,
Mischief they thrive on, each flip a delight,
Making ocean history with their funny might.

In the craft of the sea, they know just the tune,
They dance 'neath the sun, think they're 'way past noon,
With tails swishing wide, they unwind and relax,
Crafting some joy with their jests and their jacks.

What a comedy, cast in the brine,
Each wave is a punchline, perfectly fine,
As laughter soars high, through waters so clear,
In the joyous splash, all their friends cheer.

Echoes of the Tides

In the splash of sunlit waves,
A fin pops up, then quickly braves.
With a flip and flop, they play a game,
Making fish laugh, can't feel the shame.

They dance a jig with leaps and spins,
Water ballet where cheer begins.
Bubbles rise like giggles loud,
Joyful antics, a splashy crowd.

Whispers echo in salty air,
As they race with a cheeky flair.
The sea's a stage, and they're the stars,
Making us smile from near and far.

A friendly nudge, a watery wink,
In the depths, they plot and think.
Splashing around, they break the rules,
Masters of laughter, this crew of fools.

Graceful Spirits of the Deep

With a twist and a turn, they zoom around,
In underwater games, they're joyfully crowned.
A flick of the tail, a sardine sigh,
As they weave through bubbles, oh my, oh my!

They chatter and chirp beneath the waves,
Daring each other, too funny to braves.
In circles and spirals, they twirl and glide,
A joyful parade in the ocean wide.

Pop up for air with a splash and a splash,
Practicing tricks that come with a crash.
With each silly dive and rolling spin,
A laugh from the ocean, a cheer from within.

They find seaweed hats, it's party time,
Wearing their treasures, oh how they rhyme.
Under the sun, with glee they prance,
In a world where every wave has a chance.

Wind and Water's Embrace

The breeze blows soft, the water plays,
With leaps and bounds in sunny rays.
They glide with grace, a humorous twist,
In a world where joy cannot be missed.

With fins that flap like silly hands,
They ride the waves in laughter bands.
Chasing shadows and playful ghouls,
In deep blue waters, they break the rules.

A gust of wind, a wink from the sky,
They hug the surf, oh me, oh my!
With flips and flops, they frolic around,
Each splash a giggle, each bubble profound.

The sun smiles wide as they spin and swirl,
In a frothy whirl, they twirl and twirl.
Nature's jesters, in their grand spree,
Creating ripples of joy, wild and free.

PlayfulPods in Motion

In the shimmering sea, they bounce and leap,
Outrageous stunts, in laughter they steep.
With a splash and a giggle, they zoom on by,
Making waves dance, oh me, oh my!

Nibbling on seaweed, a crunchy delight,
Every bite shared brings joy to the night.
Cheeky companions, their smiles include,
Turning the ocean into a jolly mood.

Rolling and tumbling, a comedic sight,
A slapstick show in the fading light.
With antics so silly, they bring the cheer,
Casting away worries, replacing with sear.

So here's to the jesters, the merry and bright,
In aquatic antics, they soar to new heights.
With fins in the air, they dance with such ease,
In a rippling theatre of joy and of tease.

Dancing Shadows on the Water

The fish are laughing as they swim,
While shadows dance on a whim.
Bubbles rise like silly hats,
Splashing joy and playful chats.

A starfish twirls in a silly spin,
While clowns in shells join in the grin.
Octopuses juggle with great flair,
As the seaweed sways without a care.

Waves are giggling, what a sight,
Tickling toes in the pale moonlight.
Splashing and dashing, the sea creatures tease,
Turning a still night into a spree.

With every splash, a wild surprise,
Flipping through the sea like acrobatic flies.
Underwater, mischief floats with ease,
Where laughter echoes like the melody of the seas.

Chasing Currents

In the current, a race we'll start,
With bubbles soaring, a true work of art.
Fish high-five as they zip and zoom,
Creating whirlpools of laughter and boom.

A seahorse in sneakers dashes past,
While jellyfish glow in a disco blast.
Turtles on scooters glide with delight,
Chasing the waves, feeling so light.

Splashing around, they play hide and seek,
With clams and crabs, it's the highlight of the week.
A dolphin shrieks, "Catch me if you can!"
While a shrimp does the cha-cha; oh, what a plan!

With a cannonball, the sea stars cheer,
As fins and flippers bring joy without fear.
In the currents, we dart and spin,
Finding the fun that swims beneath the grin.

Sails and Tails

On a boat with sails bright and large,
We hear the jellyfish's silly charge.
Tails wagging like flags in a breeze,
As the ocean giggles, teasing with ease.

A witty pelican drops a fish treat,
While seagulls laugh at their own goofy feat.
Sailing along with laughter so grand,
The ocean's a circus, a joyful band.

Waves tossing up their feathery splashes,
Fish prancing 'round in their quick little flashes.
The captain's hat takes a jaunty trip,
As laughter sails on every wave and dip.

With a wink from the sun, we glide and sail,
Singing along to the ocean's tale.
In this watery world, the fun never fails,
As we dance with the wind, our spirits set to prevail.

Beyond the Horizon

Look beyond where the sea meets the sky,
With quirky critters that leap and fly.
A manta ray with laser beams,
Plays hopscotch with our wildest dreams.

A quirky crab in fancy shoes,
Struts along like he's got nothin' to lose.
The horizon giggles, a laugh so bright,
Where every wave is a cheeky delight.

As pelicans dive with exaggerated flair,
Decking the ocean with a flip and a pair.
Beneath the waves, there's a ruckus of fun,
Where the sea's a jester, second to none.

Adventures await just beyond our sight,
With the sun winking down, spreading its light.
In this place where silliness thrives,
The ocean beckons—come, take a dive!

Whispers of the Ocean's Choir

Bubbles rise with giggles near,
Fish swim by, wearing a sneer.
Splashing joy in every wave,
Seashells laugh, they love to rave.

Crabs don hats, they dance and jive,
An octopus learns how to drive.
Turtles race on tiny boards,
While seaweed plays the sweetest chords.

Starfish twirl on sandy floors,
They breakdance by the ocean shores.
A shark hums tunes, a show-off vast,
But whales just wish the fun would last.

Splashing drummers keep the beat,
With every wave, they're on their feet.
Underwater, laughter flies,
As mermaids toast to sea-bound pies.

Skyward Dances of the Sea

Breezy flips and salty flips,
Clumsy seals do belly slips.
Porpoises jump with silly grace,
While gulls engage in aerial chase.

A sea turtle lost its cap,
Stumbled 'round on a sea-slap.
Jellyfish float like balloons,
Giving fish all the best tunes.

Clownfish wear the worst of styles,
Bob up, down, with comical smiles.
Their colorful stripes all mismatched,
In the ocean, they're quite attached.

Knotted seaweed, a funny throne,
With fish that giggle, all on their own.
In ocean's dance, we find delight,
As waves keep swirling, oh what a sight!

Echoes of the Liquid Horizon

Waves whisper tales of fishy chats,
Sea cucumbers wearing hats.
The ocean floor, a stage for cheer,
While crabs conduct the orchestra near.

A narwhal thinking it's a unicorn,
Chasing echoes of a siren's horn.
Whales perform a splashy show,
Splashing everyone down below.

A bubble party in the sun,
With sea stars laughing, oh what fun!
Anemones sway, giving hugs,
As the ocean joins the dances and shrugs.

With flippers flapping, they take the lead,
All the fish follow, yes, indeed!
Underneath, a giggling spree,
The liquid horizon, wild and free.

Aquatic Dreams on the Wind

In the surf, a dolphin frolics,
Doing tricks that look ironic.
Whispers of laughter fill the air,
As sea life turns into a fair.

A shrimp twerks on a sandy stage,
Dad crabs cheer, full of rage.
Clownfish joke with silly quips,
While starfish try to do backflips.

Sardines glide in a tight formation,
Creating waves of strange elation.
With jellyfish floating like confetti,
The ocean's a dance—splashy and ready.

In big bubbles, tales are spun,
Silly secrets, lots of fun.
As squids squirt ink like a painter's brush,
In aquatic dreams, we feel the rush.

Ballet of the Brine and Breeze

With tails that flip and splash,
They dance in joyful spree,
A pirouette of fishy fun,
As waves sing merrily.

Giddy friends in watery gowns,
They twirl 'neath the sun's embrace,
Each leap a giggle in the surf,
A smile on every face.

The seaweed sways in tune,
To their playful ballet,
Cartwheeling through the foam,
They laugh while they frolic away.

In this liquid stage of dreams,
The audience joins the jest,
With seagulls clapping their wings,
For the performers are the best!

Sonic Echoes of Oceanic Laughter

Echoes ring through the tides,
As bubbles burp with glee,
A chorus of giggles below,
From creatures wild and free.

They play tag with the waves,
In a game of swirling sound,
While fish roll their eyes around,
At joy so tightly wound.

Splashing jokes that never end,
The sea, a vast delight,
Each wave a punchline tossed,
In nature's own comedy night.

With laughter bouncing everywhere,
And fins that flip and flop,
They create a symphony,
That no one wants to stop!

Shimmers of Joy in the Wind's Embrace

A shimmer glints in salty air,
As jests dance on foamy crests,
The breeze carries giggles forth,
A treasure chest of jest.

With every splash a chuckle bubbles,
As fins whack water's skin,
The tide collects their mirthful sound,
Where fun and joy begin.

The sunbeams join the frolic,
Spreading warmth to each soft wave,
As they waltz through the blue,
It's laughter that they crave.

Bound to mischief and to joy,
In this chilling dreamlike space,
They spin, they flip, they whistle tunes,
In a whirl of bright embrace!

Skylines of Aquatic Grace

In graceful arcs, they soar and dive,
Painting rainbows on the sea,
Each leap a tune, a rhythm found,
As joyful as can be.

The skylines shimmer with their charm,
Beneath a cerulean dome,
While waves applaud their daring stunts,
A splashy, cheeky home.

With antics bold and laughter loud,
They frolic like a dream,
Taking turns in their grand show,
An ocean's playful team.

As seafarers watch, their jaws agape,
At stunts that make hearts race,
These masters of the ocean's art,
Bring smiles to every face!

Serene Aquatic Ballet

In the shimmering tide, they twirl and sway,
Their graceful antics, a carefree display.
With flips and giggles, they glide and play,
Who knew fish could dance in such a way?

They somersault high, then splash with a cheer,
Making waves of laughter, oh what a year!
Noses poke up, as they eye us near,
A circus of smiles, with nothing to fear.

Fins wave like flags in the sun's bright light,
They chuckle in bubbles, a delightful sight.
Every leap feels like pure delight,
Keeping our hearts free, soaring in flight.

With a wink and a nod, they tease the sea,
Playing peekaboo, as spry as can be.
Their joy contagious, wild and carefree,
In this splashy ballet, we're all filled with glee.

Silver Shadows Beneath the Sky

Under gleaming waves, laughter unfurls,
Where silver shapes twirl, like spun-up pearls.
With playful nudges, they chase little swirls,
An underwater party, the ocean twirls.

Shadows flit by, as they spin and dive,
Bubbles burst forth, as they come alive.
In the sea's embrace, their spirits thrive,
An endless ballet, where joys arrive.

Corkscrew giggles and dolphin pranks,
Whimsical dances, with no room for thanks.
They're jesters of water, filling up banks,
As waves of laughter fill the silvery flanks.

From the ripples above, we watch their fun,
Making a splash, under the wide sun.
In skies above, their antics run,
With smiles so bright, who could weigh a ton?

Joyful Leaps and Laughter

From deep ocean floors, they shoot up high,
Like rockets of joy, they cut through the sky.
With flips and grins, they are bound to fly,
Their laughter is contagious, oh my, oh my!

Leaping with zest, their spirits ignite,
Splashing the surface, what a sheer delight.
In their playful world, everything's bright,
It's a game of joy, endless and light.

Chasing the bubbles, racing the sun,
Who could resist such adorable fun?
With squeals of mirth, they're never done,
In the watery playground, they're number one.

As spectators, we watch with pure glee,
Their playful antics are a sight to see.
Each leap, a reason for a chuckle spree,
In this world of laughter, we all feel free.

Currents of Freedom

Waves crinkle and gleam, as they zoom through the spray,
With the joy of the sea, they dance and play.
Twists and turns in a slippery ballet,
Freedom a splash, as they frolic away.

With tails that swish, they create a delight,
Rolling and tumbling, spirits so bright.
In sparkling waters, they leap with might,
A comedy show, within our sight.

Their laughter echoes, soft as the breeze,
Filling the ocean with joyous decrees.
In playful pursuits, they drift with ease,
Bringing forth chuckles, like rippling lees.

With every splash, they give a grand cheer,
Inviting us close, to share in the sheer.
Their freedom contagious, lifting all fear,
In wild water antics, we all hold dear.

Whirls of Joy beneath Sunlit Skies

In the splash of waves, they twist and glide,
A circus act where laughter can't hide.
With flips and spins, they steal the show,
Winking at clouds, putting on a glow.

Belly flops send seaweed flying high,
Bubbly giggles that echo and sigh.
They tease the seagulls, a cheeky parade,
Making fish jump, all jokes well played.

Sun hats float by in the playful spray,
It's a wild surf party, hip-hip-hooray!
With squeals and splashes, they dance in the light,
Just ocean jesters, a whimsical sight.

In the warmth of the sun, all worries flee,
As joy rides the waves, in pure comedy.
In whirlpools of laughter, we find our cheer,
These aquatic clowns bring summer near.

Nautical Serenade on the Horizon

Under the sun, a frolic begins,
With tails of silver, where the laughter spins.
They sing to the tide, in a cheeky tone,
Making waves while calling the sea their own.

Wobbling and bobbing, they chase the spray,
Making bubbles burst in a silly ballet.
With splashes like music, they play their part,
Each flip and dive, a piece of their art.

Seaweed wigs that twist on their heads,
Pretending to dance on invisible threads.
A comedy show with a salty refrain,
As they glide through water, joy can't contain.

From sunset to dawn, the giggles take flight,
In nautical rhymes, they spread pure delight.
With a wink and a splash, they steal our hearts,
Creating a symphony where laughter starts.

Spirit Splash: Days of Leisure

In the gentle waves, they plot and play,
With playful nudges that brighten the day.
A splash here and there, like confetti around,
With joyful leaps, they dance from the ground.

Their flips are a jest, a comic display,
With playful shrieks that keep boredom at bay.
Seaweed crowns perched at the tips of their fins,
They parade through the surf, where the laughter begins.

With the sun sparkling bright like a comedy gem,
These frolicsome spirits are the heart of the hem.
A flirt with the tides, a tickle of foam,
In the ocean's embrace, they feel right at home.

As sunset kisses water, they share their delight,
In the whispers of waves, they dance through the night.
With giggles that scatter like shells on the shore,
Spirit of leisure, they give us much more.

Gale-Kissed Rhapsody of the Ocean

Where the winds do whistle, a tune we can't miss,
The playful ones frolic, in joyous bliss.
With tails that flick like a comical shoot,
In watery antics, their spirits take root.

As gusts of laughter blow past our ears,
They skirt through the waves, conquering fears.
Each swish and a splash, a jest in the blue,
With smiles that echo, they welcome us too.

In whirlwinds of cheer, they spin with delight,
These merry sea spirits, a wondrous sight.
They ride on the breeze, with grins ear to ear,
In a gale-kissed rhapsody, joy's crystal clear.

As moonlight reflects on their playful parade,
They dive into laughter, a summertime charade.
In waves of amusement, they beckon us near,
With breezy shenanigans, they make it all clear.

Aquatic Dreams

Underwater acrobats play,
Bouncing bubbles all the way.
Flipping fish with silly grins,
Splashing in as laughter wins.

Seaweed hats on every head,
Jellyfish bounce on shoals of bread.
The octopus can't find his shoe.
He dances odd, it's quite a view.

A crab wearing shades of blue,
Struts along like he's brand new.
Starfish cheering from their perch,
Joining in with rhythmic lurch.

Turtlenecks for turtles, oh my!
Cracking jokes as they swim by.
Underwater, jokes do swim,
Who knew the sea was full of whim?

Soaring Over the Surf

Flip and flop, a finned parade,
Surfboards carved from beachside jade.
Seagulls chuckle at the sight,
Waves of laughter, pure delight.

A fish in sunglasses, oh so cool,
Rides the wave, staying in school.
The sea cucumber holds its breath,
Wishing for a regal death.

A hermit crab, a tiny dream,
Wears a conch, it's quite the scheme.
The dolphin asks, "Can I get a ride?"
While sandcastles flounder with pride.

Whales sing tunes, a silly show,
As sea snails dance nice and slow.
The ocean's mirth, an endless spree,
Where laughter bubbles wild and free.

Twilight's Water Ballet

The ocean dons a twilight gown,
As fishes twirl and spin around.
Seagulls tap-dance on the tide,
While starbeams giggle, swell with pride.

Moonlight sprinkles dance on waves,
Crabs go wild, acting like knaves.
Whirls of foam, a swirling spree,
"Who's the best?" they laugh with glee.

A seal in a beret so chic,
Winks a fin as he takes a peak.
"Shall I steal the show tonight?"
The audience roars in pure delight.

Ballet flounders, pirouettes grand,
Fishy prance to the sea's command.
Under the glow, fun takes flight,
In twilight's waltz, all feels just right.

Tales of the Ocean's Breeze

Once a fish dreamed of the sky,
Wearing wings to sail and fly.
He leaped right up but fell back down,
Kicking up a bubble crown.

A whale who thought he could compete,
In a sprint, oh what a feat!
With laughter ripple through the sea,
"I'll stick to singing, let it be!"

Clams whisper tales of buoyant charm,
While starfish clap with leafy arm.
The seahorse laughs, tail swirls in glee,
Joking about fish that wish to flee.

And so the ocean spins its yarns,
Filled with giggles, charm, and charms.
A world where every splash is fun,
And underwater, joy's never done.

Reflections of a Skipping Heart

In the splashy sea, they prance and twirl,
With flips that make the ocean swirl.
They giggle in the salty spray,
Telling fish to join the play.

With a leap, they steal the show,
A circus act, a watery glow.
Bubbles burst like popcorn near,
While starfish clap, they cheer, they cheer!

In the sparkling sun, a dance unfolds,
Their joy like stories yet untold.
Crabs in tuxedos line the shore,
While seagulls squawk for an encore.

So let the waves tickle their toes,
As laughter twirls where the seaweed grows.
With each splash, a new jest starts,
Echoing the rhythm of skipping hearts.

Tide's Playful Waltz

Oh, the tide pulls them in for a spin,
As sea foam giggles, letting them win.
With a flip and a flop, they glide with grace,
Splashing around in a sunlit race.

The barnacles join in the jig, so spry,
While jellyfish sway like they're oh-so-high.
Each wave a chuckle, a wink, a tease,
As shells applaud in the wake of the breeze.

Seaweed becomes their joyful hat,
And starfish play tag, imagine that!
With a wink at the sun, they shake their tail,
In this ocean party, they'll never pale.

As laughter rolls in on the foamy tide,
Every splash says, "Let's go for a ride!"
In this watery waltz, they leap and they cheer,
A grand performance, with no hint of fear.

Sun-kissed Swimmers

In the dawn's golden glow, they rise with flair,
Flipping and swirling, a wild affair.
With smiles wide, they dive headfirst,
In this ocean plunge, they've quenched their thirst.

Fins waving like banners, they race the sun,
Tails flicking laughter, oh, what fun!
Starfish join in, crowns on their heads,
Spinning their tales as the ocean spreads.

With a somersault, they tease the tide,
Jumping through waves like a quirky slide.
Bubbles become popcorn, floating so free,
While mermaids sit back, just sipping their tea.

Through seaweed forests, their antics burst,
In a twirl of joy, they'll never be cursed.
A dance of delight, the ocean's spirit,
In each playful leap, you can truly hear it.

Harmony of Nature's Mischief

Whispers of waves create a tune,
As playful swimmers swirl by noon.
On fins they prance with bursts of glee,
While fish wiggle in harmony.

Every leap tells of secrets shared,
Of tricks and pranks, and laughter bared.
With a splash, they blow bubbles like gum,
As crabs in bow ties come join the fun.

From coral to floor, they twirl and glide,
In this dance of life, they take such pride.
Fins flipping high, they give a shout,
As dolphins giggle, there's never a doubt.

Nature's mischief in this playful chase,
With a shake of the tail, they find their space.
In the ballet of tides, joy skips around,
In the heart of the ocean, laughter is found.

Dance of the Sea Spirits

With flips and splashes, they beguile,
A frolicsome frolic, full of style.
Their laughter echoes, a bubbly cheer,
As they pirouette without a fear.

They twirl and swirl in the salty air,
Making seaweed wigs, what a hair!
A tap-dance on waves, oh what a sight,
With giggles that shimmer in the moonlight.

Belly flops in unison, quite a scene,
A watery circus, so bold and keen.
They jest with the turtles, in playful tease,
A splashy ballet among the seas.

In rhythm they sway, on currents they glide,
Nature's own jesters on a buoyant ride.
With every leap, a comedy's born,
As sea spirits dance till the break of dawn.

Breeze-Carried Laughter

The wind whispers secrets, a ticklish breeze,
Sea-sprites giggle, with joyous ease.
They play peek-a-boo with the fish so bright,
Turning the ocean into pure delight.

A game of tag, in shimmering waves,
These cheeky sprites are real sea knaves.
With splashes and squeaks, they sing their tune,
Under the watchful eye of the moon.

They ride on ripples, like flapping sails,
Telling fishy tales that tickle and trail.
Flipping and flopping, a quirky show,
A waving curtain, and off they go!

Their humor is caught like driftwood in tide,
A whimsical wave where giggles abide.
With a wink and a nod, they invite a cheer,
With every laugh, the ocean draws near.

Woven Currents

In strands of foam, they weave a plot,
Sprightly waves in their sunny spot.
A tapestry of laughter, brightly spun,
Where every splash is just pure fun.

Clapping their fins in playful delight,
Merging with currents, oh what a sight!
Rolls of giggles, like pearls they chase,
A frothy parade in a watery race.

Skip and swerve, like a swimmy dance,
They twirl and whirl in a frothy trance.
Knocking 'round bubbles, they laugh with glee,
In a world of wonder, wild and free.

With every glide, a joke is spun,
The ocean's jesters, who dance and run.
They intertwine laughter, like ribbons of blue,
In the woven currents, a prank or two.

The Sky's Water Play

Bouncing on waves like a bouncy ball,
Under the glimmer of sun's bright call.
Giggling chasers in a splashy spree,
They dart and dive, in joyous glee.

With little backflips that steal the show,
And silly spins that steal the flow.
A high-five with waves, a cheeky plight,
Making merry mischief in pure delight.

Their antics spark like stars at sea,
Frothy giggles like bubbles flee.
They play tag with the tide, what a riot,
A drenching delight, pure water diet!

From horizon's stretch to the break of foam,
They frolic and flip, in their salty home.
With each little splash, a laugh unashamed,
In the sky's water play, fun is proclaimed.

Freedom in a Splash

In the sea, they twist and twirl,
With flips and tricks, they make us whirl.
A splash so grand, they tease the shore,
Just when we think we've seen it all!

Salty hair and laughing glee,
They surf the waves, wild and free.
Chasing fish like they've gone mad,
Who knew the ocean was this rad?

They race the boats, a cheeky game,
With squeaks and clicks, they call our name.
Belly flops make everyone cheer,
These jokers of the sea, oh dear!

When the sun sets, they gather round,
With stories of the waves they found.
In cozy pods, they chat and play,
Who wouldn't want to join their day?

Clear Water Explorers

In waters clear, they dance and glide,
With playful jumps, they take great pride.
They pop their heads out, give a grin,
And say, "Hey there, come join the fun!"

Adventurers of the ocean blue,
With silly tricks, they'll entertain you.
A spin and splash, they'll have you gasping,
While seagulls watch, envious, clasping.

"What's that over there?" they chatter loud,
As fish parade, they feel so proud.
Their curiosity is hard to beat,
Every day's a playful retreat!

In harmonious waves, they sing their song,
Together they dance, all night long.
With twinkling eyes and laughter bright,
These jesters make the ocean light!

Ocean's Song

With a flip and a splash, they steal the show,
As if they're putting on a grand rodeo.
Their squeaks and whistles add to the tune,
Who needs a band when you have this boon?

They chase the currents with comic flair,
Balancing seaweed, unaware of a scare.
With jellyfish tags for their next dance move,
These clowns of the ocean always improve!

When the tide rolls in, they turn their tails,
Racing each other, who never fails.
They flip over waves, creating a fuss,
While ocean critters ride the bus!

Undersea jesters, kings of the play,
Each jump ignites a sunny ballet.
Their laughter echoes, a joyful ring,
In the ocean's heart, they still dance and sing!

Celestial Swimmers

In moonlit waters, they twinkle and twist,
With antics that make the stars just insist.
They dance in circles, a shimmering sight,
Making the ocean feel so light!

With starfish hats and seaweed ties,
They float through the night, oh what a surprise!
Stellar hugs and bubbly cheers,
As they invite us near, their joy steers!

Giggling with bubbles, spinning like tops,
In this deep blue, the fun never stops.
"Catch me if you can!" they giggle and race,
Creating ripples, leaving trace.

So here's to the jesters of aquatic delight,
Under the moon dazzling bright.
With each gleeful flip and sparkling dive,
They keep the ocean's spirit alive!

Surfing with the Spirits

On waves they hop with glee,
Spirits laughing, wild and free.
With water sprayed like foam,
They dance and twirl, no need for home.

They've got style as they glide,
With goofy grins, they ride the tide.
Waking seas with a playful splash,
Surfing humor, making a splash!

As seagulls caw and dive,
These jokers thrive, feel alive.
With a flip and a twist that's grand,
They pull off stunts, oh so planned!

So next time you see waves unfold,
Remember the stories that's been told.
Of spirits wild, fun on the crest,
Surfing with spirits, they're the best!

Bubbles and Breeze

In the sun, they blow some bubbles,
Swirling 'round without any troubles.
With snickers and giggles in the air,
They send giggly ripples everywhere.

A bubble floats, then pops with a cheer,
Making room for others to appear.
Wobbling with laughter, they spin and glide,
In a breeze of chuckles, oh what a ride!

Down below, the fish swim near,
Eyebrows raised, they join in the cheer.
Mischief mingling with every dive,
Bubbles and giggles, feeling alive!

In frothy seas, they play a tune,
Dancing and laughing under the moon.
A world of giggles, they create,
Bubbles and breeze, oh, isn't it great!

Celestial Prancers

Under starlight, they take the floor,
With twirls and jumps, oh what a score!
Prancers of the ocean, bold and bright,
Moonlit dances, a pure delight.

With a flip and a twirl under the sky,
Cosmic humor, they wink and fly.
Their fins a-flutter, tails in a spin,
Making waves with a cheeky grin!

Galactic grooves, swirling wide,
Caught up in a heavenly tide.
With laughter bubbling, their spirits soar,
Celestial jesters, forevermore.

Through night's embrace, they roam in glee,
Stars above, glistening sea.
In cosmic capers, they find their way,
Prancing and laughing till break of day!

Whispering Tails

In the deep where secrets swim,
Whispers travel on a silvery whim.
Tails that flick, tales that tease,
Beneath the surface, they dance with ease.

With a flick and a flap, they weave their play,
Joking lines, in every sway.
A whisper here, a chuckle there,
Joyful echoes fill the air!

Through coral gardens, they glide so free,
Whispering jokes, a giggling spree.
They twist and turn, with laughter bright,
In waves of giggles, pure delight!

So when you hear a splash and a cheer,
Know that the jesters have gathered here.
With whispers and tails, they make their art,
Creating joy from the depths of the heart.

Love Letters from the Sea's Heart.

In a bottle, a note sets sail,
Packed with giggles and a fishy tale.
The octopus scribbles, with much finesse,
While clams drop hints in a seabed dress.

The starfish writes with a thumb so wide,
Scribbling secrets where shellfish hide.
A sea turtle giggles, his pen so slow,
He takes a nap, and the ink starts to flow.

Fish read letters in a bubble of light,
"Hey, krill! Let's party! It's a wild night!"
They swim in circles, with much delight,
Makin' a splash 'til the morning light.

So if you find a message of glee,
Remember the fun in the wild, blue sea!
It's a world of laughter, no need to fret,
Just keep on swimming; there's more to get!

Ocean Dancers

Bubbles bouncing, the seabed's alive,
With fish in tutus, they gracefully dive.
A crab DJ spins on a rock so grand,
While seaweed sways to the ocean band.

Turtles twist with a gentle sway,
In a conga line, leading the ballet.
Jellyfish waltz, with their tentacles bold,
Chasing the laughter, their stories unfold.

Clownfish giggle, they're the life of the show,
With tiny top hats, they put on a glow.
It's a dance-off, a splashy parade,
In the blue ballroom where friendships are made.

So come to the dance, don't just be a viewer,
Join in the fun, become a sea breather.
The ocean's alive with a rhythm so sweet,
Dance with the waves and move to the beat!

Symphony of the Sea

A whale choir starts with a booming tune,
Echoing softly beneath the bright moon.
While snails play violins made out of shells,
The anemones hum sweet oceanic bells.

A crab plays drums on a coral stone,
With clapping clams singing in a happy tone.
The seaweed sways like a flutist's hand,
Creating a magic across the vast sand.

Bubbles burst in rhythm, such a playful sound,
As fish form a chorus, swimming 'round and 'round.
With barnacles tapping, they keep time right,
In the symphony's heart, where dreams take flight.

So hear the ocean's song, so bright and clear,
It's a concert of laughter for all who are near.
Join in the fun, bring your giggle and cheer,
Let the sea's sweet harmony fill you with cheer!

Whispers of the Waves

The waves murmur secrets to the sandy shore,
"Did you see that dolphin? He made us roar!"
They gossip of fish in fancy attire,
Dressed in their glittery scales, they aspire.

"Oh, that starfish thinks he's a real cool dude,
Wearing sun hats made from kelp, oh so shrewd!"
The shimm'ring shells chime in with a laugh,
As sea cucumbers shake in their colorful craft.

Little crabs chuckle, making pinching jokes,
While jellyfish giggle at their glowing pokes.
The sea grass dances, whispering delight,
Telling tales of the creatures that bubble at night.

So lean in, dear friend, hear the playful lore,
From the lips of the sea, there's always more!
Each wave brings laughter, a tickle and tease,
Join in the whispers, the world's here to please!

Horizon's Joy

A splash of laughter greets the sea,
Where finned acrobats dance with glee.
They flip and twirl, a silly sight,
Wearing their smiles, oh what a delight!

Jumps like popcorn, plops like a clown,
Twirling in circles, never a frown.
With fishy pranks, they tease and play,
In waves of laughter, they splash their way.

They race with seagulls, swift as a dart,
In a game of tag, they play their part.
Their giggles echo through ocean's tune,
As sunshine giggles at a brightened noon.

A splash here, a splash there, oh what fun!
Chasing shoals till the day is done.
With seaweed crowns and kelp as bling,
These light-hearted jesters make the waves sing.

Liquid Dreams

In azure depths, where ripples play,
A silly crew keeps gloom at bay.
With bubbles bursting, laughter sprees,
They dance to rhythms of liquid ease.

Splashing through kelp, a zany race,
With masks of sand, they love the chase.
Making waves with a cheeky grin,
Their ocean kingdom, a stage within.

Surprises abound, like fish in tights,
Twisting in whirlpools, oh what sights!
Every flip and flounder turns out right,
A comical circus, pure delight!

As currents whisper a playful tune,
They sway and spin in the light of moon.
With slosh and squirt, they steal the scene,
Creating mischief, all bright and keen.

Celestial Companions

Under the waves, stars hang around,
Where jokesters flourish, delight abound.
With winks and flips, they steal the show,
In a cosmic waltz, watch them go!

Trading tales with fish in a whirl,
Making sea foam dance and twirl.
Bouncing off bubbles, they start to prance,
A merry ballet in a blue expanse.

They twinkle like stars in an ocean vast,
Sharing cosmic giggles, having a blast.
With fins in a flurry, oh what a scene,
They sync with the tides, a splashy routine!

Celestial jesters in a liquid light,
Painting the ocean with sheer delight.
As waves applaud, they bow and grin,
In the theater of water, joy begins.

Chasing the Sunlit Surge

With morning rays, the sea awakes,
A raucous crew, no time for fakes.
Chasing the swell, they'll race the tide,
With laughter echoing, they're filled with pride.

In sun-kissed frolic, they leap and dive,
Each splash a giggle, feel so alive!
With wobbly spins and silly stunts,
The ocean's playground knows their fronts.

A swish and a swirl, off they go,
On waves of joy, they steal the show.
An aerial ballet, they rule the sea,
In a whirl of antics, so wild and free.

With twinkling eyes in the surf they play,
In sunlit surges, they frolic all day.
With flips and flops, a merry brigade,
Chasing the horizon, in laughter, they're made.

www.ingramcontent.com/pod-product-compliance
Lightning Source LLC
Chambersburg PA
CBHW062106280426
43661CB00086B/268